Divorce
The Comic Coloring Book

Grab your markers. Relief is waiting!

Look for the 5 unique "Sharing Is Caring Postcards" inside. Join the fun with our Sharing Community at www.comicdivorce.com because we all need a laugh. Pick a postcard inside and upload your story using your name or any alias you choose. It's time to click and laugh.

1. Divorce Rhyme
2. Mis-creations (Ex-law and Ex)
3. Snuggle Hunk
4. Grapevine
5. Halls of Justice

The Story

This book came about as a happy accident during a very difficult time. I was going through a divorce and asked a young man for some help to pack boxes and load them in my rented U-Haul. Enter Ian Stinson, a 25-year-old friend of the family.

As Ian and I packed, Ian chuckled as we talked about my crazy divorce. The more I talked, the more Ian laughed. Finally he said, "Debbie your divorce stories are hilarious; you should seriously write a book." My divorce case had already been a cover story on the Virginia Lawyers Weekly and named a top legal case in Virginia in 2013 and then again in 2015. I had a lot of stories.

The more I thought about Ian's suggestion, the more it seemed like a good idea. So, I began jotting down all the things that made Ian laugh. As I was recounting my experiences, they were so much more than the absurdity of my divorce proceedings and legal issues.

What I began to focus on was the enormity of change divorce brings to every part of one's life. I found that trying to find some humor in the tragedy of divorce was empowering. As I began developing images for the book, I tried to put a little humor in the real-life situations that come as a result of divorce. By doing so, I hope to give women who find themselves in similar situations some comic relief.

Remember When....
You Wanted to Know
Everything About Him?

Ding! Your Wish Came True

They say to get to really know someone, you have to divorce them. Seeing your Ex's new identity is like watching an odd fairy tale creature emerge, yet you recognize the body and face.

The History of Divorce

To understand modern day divorce, let's go back in time. King Henry VIII of England, who was married six times, devised the first divorce.

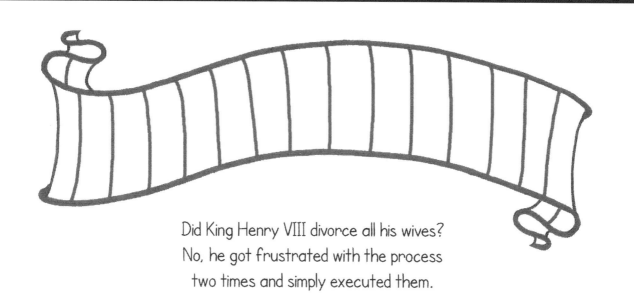

Did King Henry VIII divorce all his wives?
No, he got frustrated with the process
two times and simply executed them.
Hence, the famous rhyme:

♫ Divorced, Beheaded, Died…
    Divorced, Beheaded, Survived. ♫

Divorce has
come a long way.
At least you get
to keep your
head!

If Sharing is Caring

...then venting is reinventing. Let's help you out of the divorce dolldrums and into a better place. Create your Divorce Rhyme, which may not be famous, but it could be funny. Email a photo of your Divorce Rhyme Postcard to share@comicdivorce.com or upload using your name or any alias you choose at Our Sharing Community on www.comicdivorce.com.

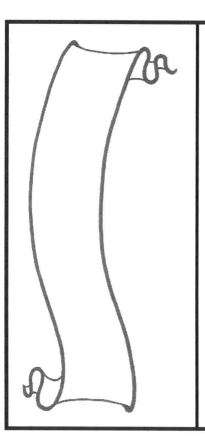

Here's an example to get you started:
The lawyer called today, things have gone astray.
My Ex said that we would always be friends, but
that all ended today...

Postcard: Your Divorce Rhyme

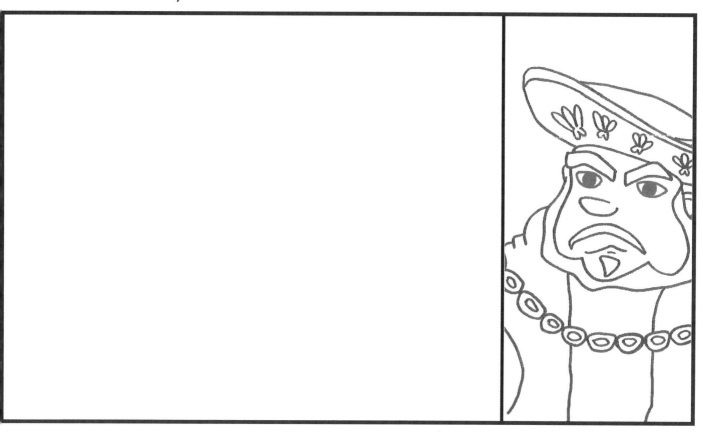

CRACKING UP.

Humpty Dumpty sat on a wall, Humpty Dumpty had a great fall. All the King's horses and all the King's men couldn't put Humpty back together again. Who needeth horses, and who needeth men™? You can put yourself back together again.

Divorce is like falling off a wall, you can break. So round up your scissors and gather your tape, in no time at all, you'll be in good shape.

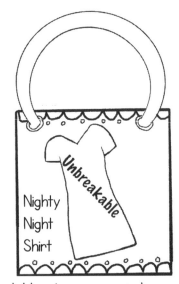

Available at www.comicdivorce.com

YOU'RE NO HUMPTY DUMPTY

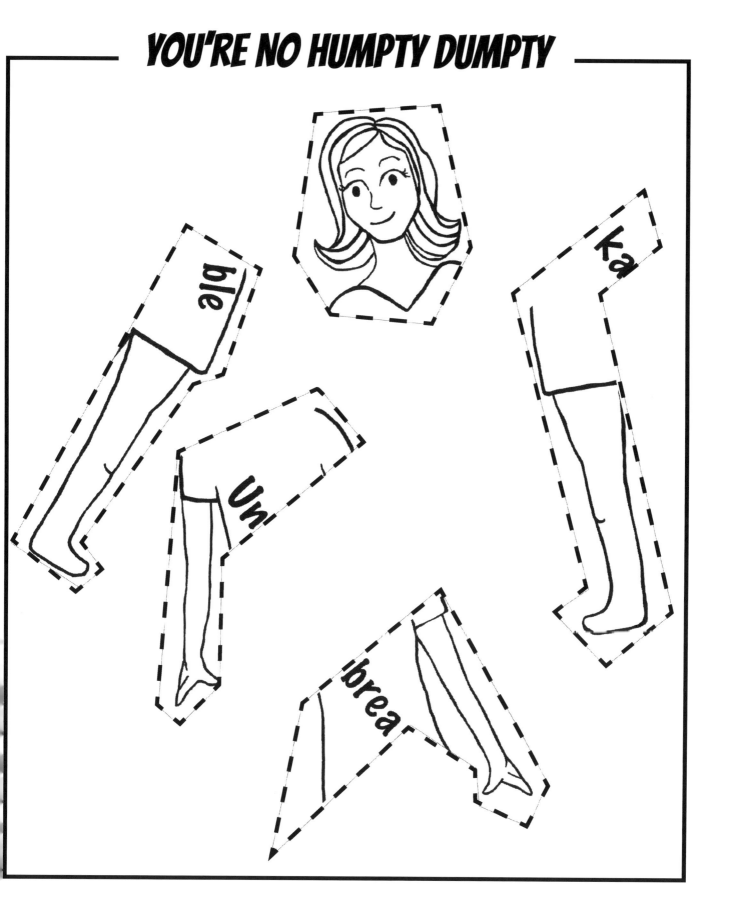

My Ex Thou Art

Here's a funny word game to vent your Ex's issues in a classical way.
If you get any of these words in your legal documents, depositions,
or better yet, a court transcript, you instantly make it into the
Comic Divorce Hall of Fame.

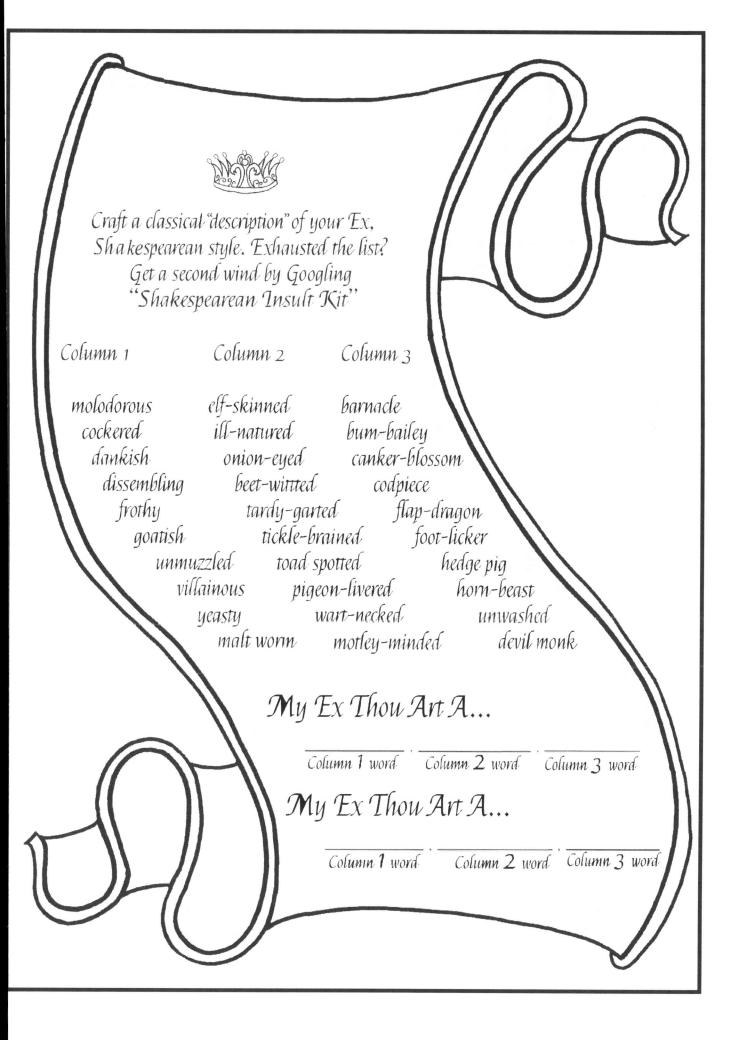

Craft a classical "description" of your Ex.
Shakespearean style. Exhausted the list?
Get a second wind by Googling
"Shakespearean Insult Kit"

Column 1	Column 2	Column 3
molodorous	elf-skinned	barnacle
cockered	ill-natured	bum-bailey
dankish	onion-eyed	canker-blossom
dissembling	beet-witted	codpiece
frothy	tardy-garted	flap-dragon
goatish	tickle-brained	foot-licker
unmuzzled	toad-spotted	hedge-pig
villainous	pigeon-livered	horn-beast
yeasty	wart-necked	unwashed
malt-worn	motley-minded	devil-monk

My Ex Thou Art A...

_____ _____ _____
Column 1 word   Column 2 word   Column 3 word

My Ex Thou Art A...

_____ _____ _____
Column 1 word   Column 2 word   Column 3 word

The Wedding Photo Dilemma: The Furry Ones

A unique problem every divorcee has to deal with. Nothing says healing like cutting and pasting. Cut your Ex's face from photos and insert into the dotted circles. There are six Ex-Animals™. Choose which one best fits your Ex, or you can complete all six.

Weasel
A fearsome predator who performs a "weasel war dance" to distract and confuse its prey.

Skunk
Even if slightly provoked, they can leave you smelly for days.

The Wedding Photo Dilemma: The Slimy Ones

Want even more fun? Take your favorite Ex-Animal™ off these pages, make them into popsicle stick puppets, use them to photo-bomb, insert them into 4x6 picture frames, etc. The options are endless.

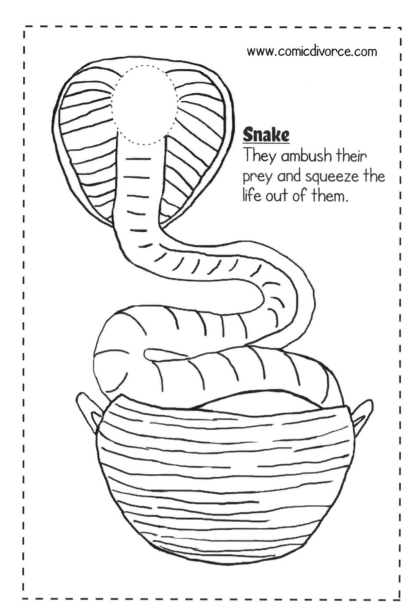

www.comicdivorce.com

Snake
They ambush their
prey and squeeze the
life out of them.

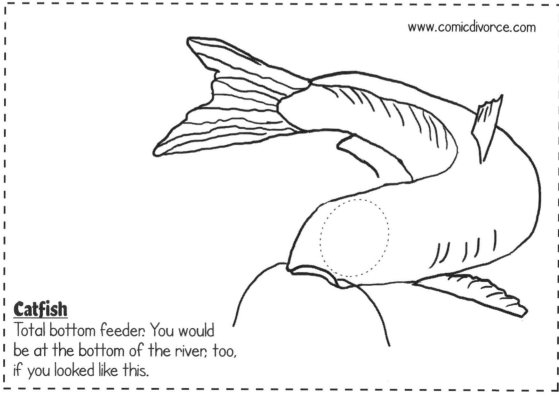

www.comicdivorce.com

Catfish
Total bottom feeder. You would
be at the bottom of the river, too,
if you looked like this.

The Wedding Photo Dilemma: The Wingers

This should be enough to help you redirect your Ex's image into something more comical. Now onto what happens when you actually have to hear him speak!

Bed Bug
Irritating. Almost impossible
to get rid of.

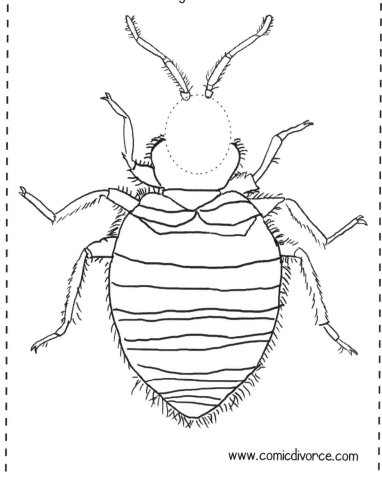

www.comicdivorce.com

Turkey
The "strut act" where
they puff out their
chests, make loud
noises, and fan out
their feathers to entice
females.

www.comicdivorce.com

DANGER! BLACK HOLE OF DARKNESS™

It's not rocket science. If your Ex's Black Hole of Darkness™ starts blasting, turn off all command communications and shut that portal down. Don't get sucked into that hole, where your mind will never come out.

I am out of here!

MIS-CREATIONS OF THE EXLAW VARIETY™

No discussions about your Ex would be complete without addressing your in-laws... whoops... we mean Ex-laws. Write whatever comes to mind of the ridiculous, outrageous, or flat-out funny things your Ex-laws or Ex have said to you or about you. It's time to send those monsters on their way. Email a photo of your Mis-creations Postcard to share@ comicdivorce.com or upload using your name or any alias you choose at Our Sharing Community on www.comicdivorce.com.

Postcard: Mis-creations

MOVING ON...

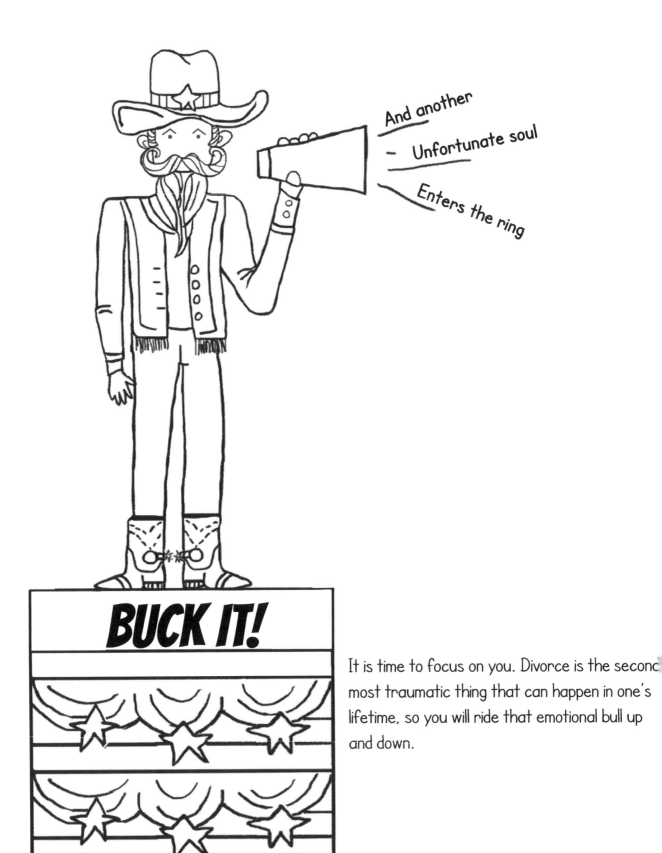

And another

- Unfortunate soul

Enters the ring

BUCK IT!

It is time to focus on you. Divorce is the second most traumatic thing that can happen in one's lifetime, so you will ride that emotional bull up and down.

HANG ON AND RIDE IT OUT!

GOT FEAR?

Turn your fear to fierce and step right up and show those ducks what you've got. You will work through it. When fear hits, remember, "All that ever holds somebody back, I think is fear. For a minute I had fear. Then I went to the dressing room and shot my fear in the face!" - Lady Gaga

Dwarfettes of Divorce™
Scene 1

Fear is not the only emotion that visits you on your whirlwind trip to Divorceland. Often the trip is like an animated movie of seven emotional dwarf characters in your head arriving and departing during the scenes of your day-to-day life. Meet Frazzled, Doc, Loopy, Crabby, Ragey, Rosey, and Mopey. They might be around for a while, but it's just a scene, let them in, and then let them out!

Dwarfettes of Divorce™ Scene 2

Of course we broke them up into two pages. Can you imagine all seven of them arriving at one time?

You're on the Right Path, Keep on Going

One more emotion, and it deserves a two-page image.
Bitterness. It's a tough one.

YOUR BODY ON DIVORCE

It's not just your mind that goes through changes, but your body does as well! Here is the main checklist.

☐ **BRAIN:** The organ you should use the most.

☐ **MOUTH:** The organ you will use the most.

☐ **CARPEL TUNNEL:** From signing endless legal docs.

☐ **HEART:** On a temporary leave of absence.

☐ **LIVER:** Your coveted wine and liquor cabinet.

☐ **YAHOO:** The organ you want to use the most.

DIVORCECTOMY™

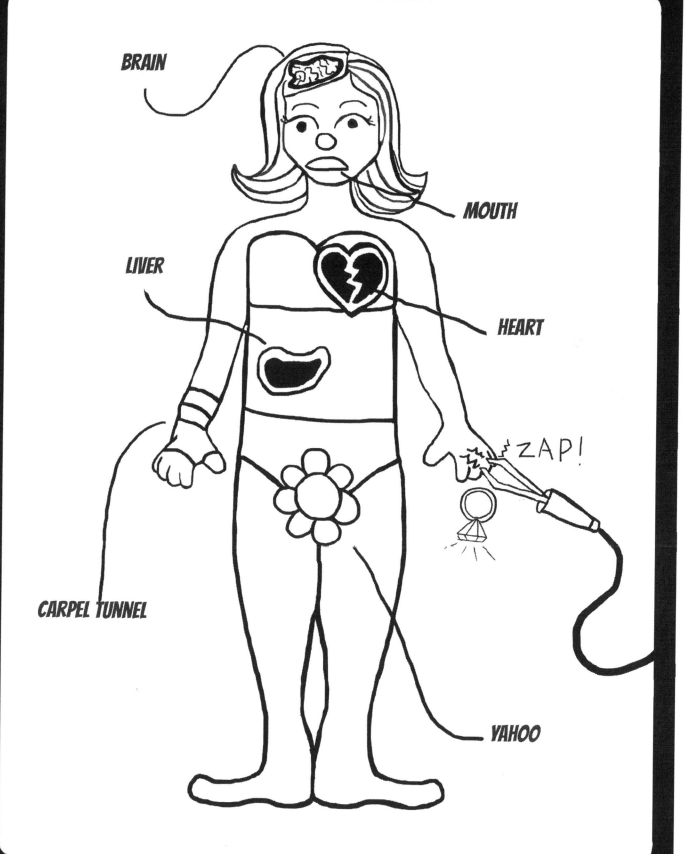

No Evil

Now that your head is in place and your body in motion, it's time to get your house in order. Implement the No Evil plan below.

Hear No Evil

Research shows music is highly beneficial for the brain. So when you feel like you're losing your mind, pull out your noise-canceling headphones, and blast your favorite tunes.

See No Evil

Remove everything that is a trigger, except drywall and electrical wiring. Trigger = anything that makes you feel sad, tired, or full of rage. Pack it up and put it away!

Speak No Evil

Speak no evil about yourself. Start with the classic SNL sketch where the actor is looking in the mirror saying, "I'm good enough, I'm smart enough, and doggonit, people like me."

Smell No Evil

Ewhh, I can still smell your Ex! Smell evokes the strongest memories, so it's time for mandatory aroma therapy in your bedroom and other trigger areas.

No Evil Candles

Available at www.comicdivorce.com

SNUGGLE HUNK™

What divorcee's bedroom would be complete without her very own Snuggle Hunk™? They say never go to bed angry, and now you don't have to. Totally therapeutic, non-confrontational, and his emotional support is endless!

Build your own Snuggle Hunk™. Start by buying a pillow and adorning it with a button-down shirt (not your Ex's). Once he is assembled, spray it with your favorite free cologne sample. If it's chilly outside, finish him off by tucking a heating pad under your Hunk's shirt. Enjoy!

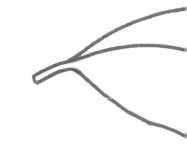

"If I were real, I would totally have sex with you."

If Sharing is Caring

...then venting is reinventing. Email a photo of your Snuggle Hunk™ and or Feather Bubble Postcard to share@comicdivorce.com or upload using your name or any alias you choose at Our Sharing Community on www.comicdivorce.com

Postcard: Feather Bubble

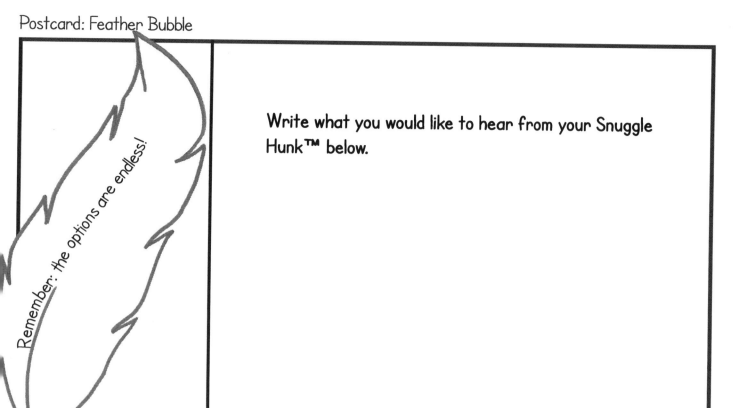

Remember: the options are endless!

Write what you would like to hear from your Snuggle Hunk™ below.

Postcard: Snuggle Hunk™

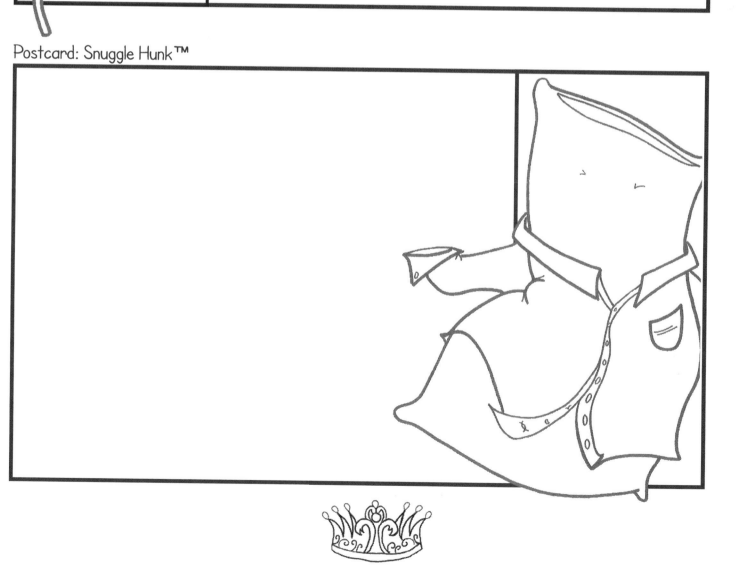

KAPOW!

There is so much to go through, including a changing social circle, dating again, and the dreaded legal issues. Here is a superhero to see you through!

28 HOUR WATCH:
Gives you an extra 4 hours each day to handle the divorce and your changing life.

BOTTLE OF WINE:
Gives you the power to enjoy events where there are only couples.

CALCULATOR:
Magically makes your finances work to buy that new dress!

TACTICAL POCKETBOOK:
Insert your hand, and it immediatley presents you with your desired item.

MASK:
Makes you fluent in many languages, most importantly Pig Latin, i.e. legalese

BOOTS:
Jetset to blast off. Allows you to escape awkward conversations.

STATUS? YOUR NEW ELEVATOR PITCH

Before divorce, you knew what to say, which included "I am married." It might be weird if you keep saying that. If you don't like the word divorce, there are infinite alternatives.

Heard it Through the Grapevine

You will speak with many people during the divorce process. Hold on to the positive ones and lose those negative ones. You don't drink nasty wine, so why hang out with nasty vines.

Nasty Vines

Great Vines

If Sharing is Caring

...then venting is reinventing. Write whatever comes to mind of the ridiculous, outrageous, or flat out funny things a "frienemy" or friend of yours has said to you or about you. Email a photo of Frienemy or Friend Postcard to share@comicdivorce.com or upload using your name or any alias you choose at Our Sharing Community on www.comicdivorce.com.

Postcard: Grapevine Frienemy

Postcard: Grapevine Friend

Dating Again

Your choice, when you are ready! Make sure to scan the lily pond before you drift, leap, or dive right in!

Halls of Justice

People dream about weddings and have nightmares about divorce. You can have a nightmare while awake, caffeinated, and fully dressed. Just watch your Ex's lawyer in front of a judge.

If Sharing is Caring

...then venting is reinventing. One thing you never hear is, "I love my Ex's attorneys." Fill in the post card with your funniest or interesting story about your legal experience. Email a photo of your Halls of Justice Postcard to share@comicdivorce.com or upload using your name or any alias you choose at Our Sharing Community on www.comicdivorce.com.

Equitable Distribution

Wishful thinking can be fun! You get to be the judge; so take your seat at the head of the E.D. scale. Finalize your ultimate deisres to help this nightmare end!

Home
for you:

_____

for your Ex:

_____

Health
for you:

_____

for your Ex:

_____

Friends
for you:

_____

for your Ex:

_____

ASSEMBLED, PROCESSED, AND DECREED

Every year over 1.2 million women ride the "Divorce Assembly Line" where they are officially Assembled, Processed, and Decreed divorced. Next time you see someone riding this line give them a hug, give them a laugh, and maybe send them a little gift to let them know they are going to make it, just like you!

And the Award Goes to You

Lots of emotions and lots of memories, but you made it through those.
Color up your award ceremony, and take a much needed break!

Hope You Enjoyed Our Cast Of Characters!

Deborah MacDougall (Author)

The ringleader that developed the concept for the Comic Book Coloring Series grew up making people laugh. Moments after Debbie started bouncing her musings off of her friends, she had an idea. Maybe looking at your divorce from an outside perspective can help you get to the point where you can laugh, not cry, at some of the trials of divorce. When coloring life into these comic images, they can add a humorous perspective to very difficult situations. Nothing would give her more happiness than to know women going through this process get a much needed laugh when coloring this book.

Ian Stinson (Co-Author)

Ian kept asking, well I have never been married, am I really qualified to do this? Who else could make Equitable Distribution even remotely funny? Only someone as kind as Ian, would have the patience to spend months working on a comic coloring book for women. When he realized we all really needed some comic relief, he offered up his comic genius. For that, we thank Ian's parents immensely for bringing him into this world and Ian for all of his talent.

W.R. MacDougall (Editor)

In-house editor, constantly barraged with content questions and asked to fine tune the visuals and message points. He was frequently woken up late at night for emergency feedback and direction.

Special thanks to Nick Kaviani
Front and back cover by Rachel Cecelski
Illustrations by Rachel Cecelski, Molly Cooper, and Maggie Gray
Book design and layout by Maggie Gray

www.comicdivorce.com

Made in the USA
San Bernardino, CA
20 February 2017